26 POEM-STORIES ABOUT ANIMALS,

A to Z, Aardvark to Zebra

Fun and Funny Poems Telling Real Stories About Real Animals

POEM STORIES BY Tom Guy Pettit

ILLUSTRATED BY Peter O'Malley Pierson

TABLE OF CONTENTS

This is a most unusual book. If you knew the author and the illustrator, you would not think they know much about kids. And you would be right. It is the first kids book either of them have done and probably the last. They are senior citizens with silver-gray hair. One is a retired marketing executive, the other a retired PhD, a professor of history. But they were kids once, too.

Author

Tom Guy Pettit

Illustrator

Peter O'Malley Pierson, Ph.D

They have watched the world for years and they do know that kids are special (especially yours); that they are curious and like fun and funny stuff, including rhythmic, rhyming poems that make them chuckle. And if those poems do a bit to satisfy or stimulate curiosity about real things in the real world, so much the better.

And they're really a lot of fun to read out loud, any verse, any poem!

So go to learn about the skunk and the skink;
one likes to slither, the other to stink!

Tom and Peter loved doing this book. They hope you and your kids don't think it stinks!

AARDVARKS AND AARDWOLVES

When you spell AARDVARK, you start with "AA"
Then "R", "D", "V", "A", "R", and finally "K"
Since "A" is the alphabet's first letter
One's good at the start, but two's even better

Aardvarks are first, so they're not often missed
On alphabetical animal lists
The creatures whose names start with just one "a"
Might think they'd go first, but that's not the way

AARDVARK

When aardvarks go to the head of the pack
Alligators and apes have to step back
And, gosh, they have to step back again
If a weirdo aardwolf wants to come in

ALLIGATOR

APE

'Cause AARDWOLF also starts out with "AA"
But it's not part aardvark in any way
They're both from Africa, that much is true
And you can find them both in many a zoo

The aardvark's like a pig – with a long snout
That sticks in the ground to get the bugs out
It traps those bugs on its long, sticky tongue
And eats them raw, which does not seem like fun

The aardwolf looks like a big ugly cat
And sleeps in its hole all day like a bat
It also eats bugs when it comes out at night
So its eyes are good, they don't need much light

AARDWOLF

For your animal list, which would you say
Ought to be first, they both start with "aa"
Is aardwolf in front and aardvark second?
Just which one goes where; what do you reckon?

As you think of the answer, you should know
They both love bugs and don't care where they go.

OH!

ANT

B

BEARS

If bears could talk and you could hear them speak
You'd learn there's a bear for each day of the week.

Monday's for Black Bears who aren't always black
That doesn't make sense, but it's a Black Bear fact
Some of 'em are brown, some white and some gray
But the black ones seem to think that's OK

Tuesday's for Grizzly Bears, what a strange name
But at least they're all colored mostly the same
Their brown fur is mixed with some that is white
And don't make them mad, they'll claw and they'll bite

Wednesday's for Brown Bears who are mostly all brown
But sometimes a yellow Brown Bear is found
Some Brown Bears are big like a cow or a horse
But you can't milk or ride a Brown Bear of course

THE STATE BROWN BEAR OF CALIFORNIA

Thursday's for Polar Bears, with fur thick and white
Like a toasty warm coat to wear day and night
It's cold where they live, so the warm coat is nice
Since they're always out in the snow and the ice

Friday's for Honey Bears, they act crazy
They're also called sloths which means they're lazy
They're sloppy and slow and slurp up honey
And burp and snort and sound pretty funny

HONEY BEARS... SLURP UP HONEY

Saturday's for the weird Spectacled Bear
They stare at you through white rings of hair
Which look a bit like glasses on their eyes
But they see OK, is that a surprise?

...LOOK A BIT LIKE GLASSES ON THEIR EYES

Sunday's for Sun Bears who sleep in the sun
In treetop nests where they seem to have fun
They have big, bright, sunny spots on their chests
You can see at night when they leave those nests

What about Koala Bears you might say
And Panda Bears too, don't they have a day?
Well, some people might say they're not real bears
But that's what they're called and nobody cares

Pandas come from China and their heads are white
But their shoulders are black, black as the night
They've got big black circles around their eyes
And black ears too, so their head's a surprise

A Koala's in fact like a Kangaroo
When you go to see one, you might see two
They're tan and carry their babies in sacks
That grow on their tummies and not on their backs

Pandas like to sit and eat bamboo
They eat lots of it, but it's hard to chew
So their teeth are big and their jaws are strong
And they can chew the bamboo all day long

Koala's eat leaves, but won't touch bamboo
But they love to sit like Pandas and chew
Eucalyptus trees grow the leaves they munch
And they eat'em all day, not just for lunch

That, my friends, is the end of this poem
But when you see bears, it's something to show'em.

SUN BEARS, WHO SLEEP IN THE SUN, IN TREETOP NESTS...

KOALA

GIANT PANDA BEAR

C

CAMELS AND THEIR HUMPS

Camels are big and have humps on their backs
And their large round feet leave humongous tracks
They mostly live where it's sandy and hot
And the wind blows that sand around a lot

Camels use water all day in the heat
But not for washing or brushing their teeth
They just drink it, that's all, lots of it, too
They'd rather stink than not drink, wouldn't you?

CAMELS DRINK, AND LOTS OF IT TOO

Riders of camels sit on the hump
Above and between the neck and the rump
They sit on saddles with handles to grab
If the ride gets rough and bouncy and bad

Camels are used where there aren't many roads
They can walk in the sand and carry big loads
You can put lots of stuff on a camel's back
From big things to small ones, from boxes to sacks

CAMEL RIDES GET ROUGH AND BOUNCY

Most camels have one hump, but some have two
You might see both kinds when you go to the zoo
Riders of two-humpers sit in the pit
Between the two humps where it's hard to fit

So two-hump camels are not as much fun
As their useful cousins who have just one
One-humpers can run as fast as a horse
They look pretty weird when they run, of course

TWO-HUMP
CAMEL
(BACTRIAN)

But they race each other like horses do
As fast as they can for a mile or two
And in those countries where camels are from
People love to watch when the races are run

Off go camels in the dust and the din!
While people shout for their favorite to win
The winning camels enjoy much fame
And most of the people know them by name

They're probably even shown on TV
All bathed and brushed for the people to see
With fancy crowns perched on top of their heads
And munching on goodies in flower beds

But in those hot deserts where camels hang out
For thousands of years, without any doubt
Strong backs of camels have carried the loads
That must be moved where there aren't any roads.

D

DONKEYS

Donkeys are gentle and easy to ride
They run or they walk, the rider decides
They'll go where it's flat or up hills or down
Out in the country or in any town

Most donkeys look like a small funny horse
But donkeys have much bigger ears of course
So they hear much better than horses do
And probably even better than you

They make a loud noise; it's called a bray
Their donkey friends hear it from far away
They bray back and forth, again and again
All day and all night, they bray to their friends

Donkeys are strong and can carry big loads
Or pull them in carts on all kinds of roads
Even on roads that are muddy and rough
Donkeys can carry and pull lots of stuff

Donkeys aren't choosy about what they eat
Except for the fact that they won't eat meat
They eat all kinds of grass and plants and weeds
They even eat flowers and pumpkin seeds

They eat leaves and grains and the bark from trees
They'll chew on any darned plant that they please
But when they eat, they get full pretty quick
And they know too much food will make them sick

So donkeys aren't hungry all of the time
With occasional snacks, they do just fine
Donkeys might look dumb, but they're pretty smart
They can do more than give rides and pull carts

DONKEYS ARE GENTLE AND EASY TO RIDE

THEY MAKE A LOUD NOISE IT'S CALLED A BRAY

Some farmers use them to guard herds of sheep.
They'll guard day and night, they don't need much sleep
If they have to, they will kick and they'll bray
To drive a big dog or a wolf away

And some donkeys are kept by kids as pets
Who think they're friendly as a pet can get
If you had a nice pet donkey to keep
What would you feed it and where would it sleep?

E

ELEPHANTS...
WON'T FIT IN YOUR CAR
OR UNDER YOUR BED.

ELEPHANTS

Elephants are so big they're hard to hide
Their legs are long and their bodies are wide
They've got big floppy ears and a huge head
They won't fit in your car or under your bed

There's a big weird thing where their nose should be
It sticks way out like a limb on a tree
They can make it hang down and touch the ground
Or point it up and move it around

Can you say "proboscis", that's what it's named?
But most folks call it a trunk just the same
Elephants can't tell us which name they'd choose
Or if they care about the one we use

Whatever it's called, they use it all day
For working, eating and drinking and play
They can grab things with it, and lift them too
And fill their own mouths with food to chew

They suck water up it and hold it there
Then put it in their mouths or anywhere
And then they can blow all that water out
Like a hose blows a stream a spurt or a spout

They also use it to breathe and to smell
It's their nose in a hose and works just swell
When stuff smells good, they can move it up close
And away from stuff that stinks or smells gross

Two horns stick out of elephants faces
They use'em to dig in lots of places
From mud, dirt and sand to the bark of trees
They dig with those horns anywhere they please

We've said they are horns, but we must explain
That's what they look like, but that's not their name
They're mostly called tusks, but that's a bit wrong
In fact they're just teeth that grow very long

And most elephants have twenty six more
Teeth a lot smaller than those two big horns
They hide in the mouth to do the chewing
But it's hard to see just what they're doing

Elephants are smart and they can be taught
They've got big brains and remember a lot
They can learn to dance on their two back feet
When they hear a lively musical beat

They can carry people and logs and things
And pick up a bell whenever it rings
They can pull big sleds and wagons and carts
And they learn where to go and when to start

But elephants are not as smart as you
They can't learn a lot of the things you do
They can't read or talk and they sure can't write
Or learn it's important to be polite.

ELEPHANTS... CAN CARRY PEOPLE
AND LOGS AND THINGS

F

FROGS

Frogs are amazing and they're fun to watch
They might make you think that they play hopscotch
That's because they jump everywhere they go
Like a bouncing ball that never goes slow

And if they're not jumping, they just sit down
Not stretching, scratching or looking around
They stay as still as a bump on a log
So it's sometimes quite hard to watch a frog

Most frogs live in puddles and lakes and ponds
So they can stay pretty wet all day long
They hide among green plants in the water
Keepin' their cool as the days get hotter

And when they're hiding, not moving at all
Their eyes are watching the bugs fly and crawl
If one gets too close, a frog will have fun
Trapping that bug with its long, sticky tongue

The frog's tongue moves quick, all sticky and wet
To snatch and eat every bug it can get
Frogs love raw bugs and they eat a whole bunch
You might call that gross, but they think it's lunch

If you see a frog as it sits and hides
So quiet and still as a stone besides
Watching for bugs to come crawling around
You might be surprised when it makes a sound

Yes, frogs often make quite a lot of noise
And that sound is mostly made by the boys
They call all the girls and when some respond
They'll call back and forth from their lakes and ponds

FROGS ARE AMAZING

10

The sound they make is often called croaking
When a person tries it, they'll be joking
It sounds a little like someone burping
Or spooning up soup so fast they're slurping

Most frogs live in water, some live in trees
Some live in bushes and hide under leaves
But every frog's back legs are big and strong
Which is why their jumps are so high and long

Now remember, we've said most frogs are green
But green's not the only frog color that's seen
Some frogs are yellow, some pink and some brown
And some get darker when the sun goes down

A frog is funny when it croaks and jumps
Or just sits still, looking happy and plump
Or snags some bugs with its long sticky tongue
To have for dinner when the day is done.

GIRAFFES

Giraffes are tall and have very long necks
So their heads can go where no one expects
Frightened birds will fly from the tops of trees
When a giraffe pokes its head through the leaves

It's plain to see why giraffes are so tall
Their legs are long like their necks, after all
So when they stand with their heads in the air
They're the tallest animals anywhere

The tallest giraffe that's ever been found
Rose nineteen feet to its head from the ground
That's probably higher than three grown men
Up on a ladder, standing end to end

Giraffes' heads look little up there so high
With little horns pointing up at the sky
And little ears sticking out from each side
While its little brown eyes are open wide

Giraffes eat a lot of leaves, twigs and plants
Even if they're covered with bugs and ants
And sticking thorns which does not seem like fun
But giraffes don't mind 'cause they have tough tongues

They like to eat from trees by lakes and ponds
So they'll have water to drink all day long
They can raise their heads way up high to eat
Then down to gulp the water at their feet

But they usually hold their heads up high
And, of course, you must know the reason why
It's a great way to see, both far and near
And high and low from their front to their rear

GIRAFFE

Giraffes will stay quiet most of each day
But sometimes they have something to say
They can whistle and bellow, snort and moo
Sometimes they're heard whining and hissing too

They also make sounds that people can't hear
You might think that seems peculiar and queer
But many animals make sounds like that
Such as elephants, whales, dolphins and bats

So when we think giraffes aren't making noise
It might be that the girls have told the boys
To remember to keep their voices low
'Cause they don't want people like us to know.

H

HIPPOPOTAMUS

When you look at a hippopotamus
You'll probably become quite curious
Why does an animal so big and strong
Want to hide in the water all day long?

But, first, there's a fact you might like to know:
Most folks prefer to just call 'em "hippo"
Hippo's a name that's quite easy to say
So we hope the hippos think it's OK

Yes, hippos hang out in water a lot
It's their way to stay cool when days are hot
But they will come out when the sun goes down
Finding grass to eat as they walk around

In the rivers and streams hippos like best
The water's not deep where they stand and rest
With just their noses and eyes sticking out
So they can breathe and sniff and look about

A hippo looks like a humongous pig
Its head and its belly are both quite big
Its legs might be short, but they're strong and thick
So hippos run fast and they sure can kick!

They can run much faster than men of course
And even almost as fast as a horse
But hippos can't go far when running fast
They're soon out of breath, so the run won't last

A group of hippos is known as a pod
Don't you think that sounds a little bit odd?
When it's horses or cows, they're called a herd
But it's "pod", not "herd", that's the hippo word

HIPPOPOTAMUS

A pod of hippos can be a surprise
When all you see are their noses and eyes
Sticking out of water, looking at you
As you wonder what they're going to do

But they will probably just stand and stare
Looking half asleep in the sun's hot glare
While sloshing water is keeping them cool
Up to their backs in a big muddy pool

But if you happen to see hippos yawn
You'll see their huge tongues, which are wide and long
We don't know why, but their jaws are huge too
Since the grass they eat is easy to chew

Hippos are grumpy and don't want to play
They'll fight anything that gets in their way
They're big and they're mean, they're creatures to fear
So people should never let them come near

The best place to see them, of course, is the zoo
Where there's a big fence between hippos and you.

IF YOU HAPPEN TO SEE
HIPPOS YAWN

IGUANAS

IGUANA

How would you like to see an Iguana?
Some kids say "yes" but others don't "wanna"
Iguanas look weird which makes kids worry
And they're not cute or cuddly or furry

Iguanas slither and creep all around
With their bellies sliding across the ground
As they crawl and snoop for something to eat
On their short, stubby legs and three-toed feet

Yes, their legs are short, but their tails are long
And hard to grab because they're thick and strong
If their tails are grabbed, iguanas will fight
Snorting and twisting and trying to bite

And sometimes they'll twist and wiggle and shake
So hard that their tails will fall off and break
And then they'll get loose and then they might grin
'Cause they know their tails will grow back again

Yes, it's true that the tail, when it's held tight
Might just come off as the iguana fights
Then the iguana can get up and go
And pretty soon its new tail will grow

Iguanas are hairless and most are green
But black ones and gray ones are sometimes seen
Some iguana boys have bright orange chests
So they look a bit brighter than the rest

Their hairless thick skin is wrinkled and rough
It looks and feels like it's dry and tough
Some of it sticks out like teeth in a line
Straight down their backs, so the lines are called spines

Some iguanas are as big as a man
And others so small they'll fit in your hand
Like birds and dogs they're not all the same size
But smaller than hippos and bigger than flies

Iguanas look grouchy, grumpy and sad
But that doesn't mean iguanas are bad
So some people even keep them as pets
And show them off to their neighbors and guests

But iguanas like to hang out in trees
Hiding while eating the berries and leaves
Or on the ground under bushes and plants
Eating the flowers the bugs and the ants

And iguanas also sure like to swim
If they see some water, they'll dive right in
They'll even dive down from high in a tree
If there's water below that they can see

Yes, iguanas can do a lot of stuff
And we hope this poem tells you enough
To decide that when you go to the zoo
You'll try to see an iguana or two.

IGUANA

J

JACKRABBITS

They've got big ears and they can run and jump
They've got huge hind legs and a skinny rump
People call their tails either black or white
But they're really just either dark or light

We bet that jackrabbits do not worry
If their tails are black or white or furry
Because jackrabbits have more things to do
Than care how their tails might look to you

They keep busy sitting still on the ground
Listening, sniffing and looking around
For animals who like to hunt for meat
And might just want a jackrabbit to eat

If such an animal sneaks up too near
The jackrabbit will most certainly hear
And will, of course, see it and smell it too
Then what would a careful jackrabbit do?

If you say they'd run, you would be right on
Boom! In a flash they jump and then they're gone
Yes, Jackrabbits take big jumps when they run
They bounce through the air and it looks like fun

With their big hind legs they can kick so strong
That a lot of their jumps are ten feet long
They might jump to their left, then to their right
Then straight ahead till they've jumped out of sight

They're so fast they usually don't get caught
By meat-eaters who like to chase them a lot
They outrun the bobcats and dodge the hawks
And jump over the snakes that hide in the rocks

THEY'VE GOT BIG EARS

TAIL WHITE AND FURRY

Jackrabbits will never eat meat of course
They like grass and plants and eat like a horse
Some also eat shrubs and the bark from trees
While others eat cactus, sagebrush and weeds

Jackrabbits loaf around most of each day
They don't do much work and they seldom play
They quietly hide while they sit and wait
For darkness to start as the day grows late

Then they'll start moving and looking around
For places where good stuff to eat is found
And they'll then have a nice jackrabbit lunch
On the bushes, the plants and grass they munch

They will keep on eating all through the night
And have full tummies at the sun's first light
Then again they'll loaf through the afternoon
'Till the sun starts down and they see the moon

So if jackrabbits kiss their kids goodnight
It's in the morning which doesn't seem right
We mostly sleep nights and work in the day
But most jackrabbits don't do it that way.

K

KANGAROOS

When you go to look at a kangaroo
Do not be surprised if you're looking at two
Because kangaroo mommies have funny sacks
That grow on their tummies, not on their backs

And in them, they carry a kid about;
All nice and warm with its head sticking out
So when you go to look at a kangaroo,
Look down at its tummy, you might see two

There's more to learn of kangaroos of course
With their big hind legs, they kick like a horse
They run very fast and jump very high
And their big ears are pointed right up at the sky

Their front legs are weird and skinny and small
But they're more like arms than legs, after all
Kangaroos stand up when they look at you
Not down on all fours like elephants do

An adult kangaroo can be called a roo
And people will know what you mean if you do
And kangaroo kids should be called joeys
That's true whether they're girls or boys

And a kangaroo group is called a mob
Yes, a mob, not a pack, a herd or a glob
Kangaroos are fussy about what they eat
They like fruit, roots and grass, but never touch meat

Australia's home to most kangaroos
But they're also now found in hundreds of zoos
And if you can learn where Australia is
You just might pass a geography quiz.

KANGAROOS

LOOK DOWN AT ITS TUMMY,
YOU MIGHT SEE TWO.

...IF YOU CAN LEARN
WHERE AUSTRALIA IS,

21

L

LEOPARDS

Leopards are cats that run fast and climb trees
They're big and they're strong and do as they please
They've been called the best looking cats of all
But often won't learn to come when they're called

Most don't make good pets like smaller cats do
So leopards are often seen at a zoo
Locked up in big cages with meat to eat
Picking it up with the claws on their feet

If they're not in a zoo, they live on the land
Near mountains and trees and rivers and sand
Hunting animals that they need to eat
'Cause leopards like nothing better than meat

When they climb up a tree they may rest on a limb
Hoping to snooze if there's not too much wind
Like jackrabbits, leopards rest in the day
Then go out at night to hunt and to play

If their fur's got dark spots, it's yellow or white
Or it might be just black, black as the night
It's beautiful fur, so soft to the touch
But leopards don't like to be touched that much

If they're touched they might just get up and run
And chasing a leopard can't be much fun
When they're zooming away, fast as they can
They'll go twice as fast as the fastest man

And they're not just fast, they know how to swim
If they come to water, they'll dive right in
So it won't matter if they're wet or dry
Don't bother to chase'em, just say goodbye!

Some leopards do learn to be gentle and fun
If they're treated right from when they are young
Petted and pampered and handled with care
In nice safe places where they won't get scared

Young leopards are just as nice as can be
They're called cubs, and they're cute and fun to see
They're born in litters of two, three or four
And sometimes there might be one or two more

But leopards would rather be left alone
To play and learn and grow up on their own
They're lovely to watch, but love to be free
To run with the wind and climb any tree.

MOOSE

There are people who think a moose looks weird
When they see its big horns and scraggly beard
And others think a moose looks cute of course
Like a big and clumsy, curious horse

And there's something to know about that name
One moose or two moose, the name's the same
Three moose or four moose or even twenty
You'll call'em moose, no matter how many

You don't say mooses and surely not meese
Even though more than one goose are called geese
And even though we do say cows or cattle
We should never say "mooses" or "mattle"

But we can call a lady moose a cow
Or cows if there's more than one somehow
And there's more here that might make milk cows laugh
You can call any baby moose a calf

Yes, ladies are cows and babies are calves
So what is the name a male moose would have?
If you say it's bull, your answer is true
So it's bull moose, cow moose and calf moose too

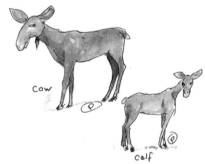

Moose eat weeds and plants and the twigs from trees
And lots of grass, just as much as they please
A cow and a calf eat less than a bull
But they'll all eat 'till their bellies are full

Grown up bull moose have big horns on their heads
Big horns that should be called antlers instead
'Cause each fall they drop off and new antlers grow
Big as the last ones and ready to go

BULL.
MOOSE

COW

Calf

24

Moose have two cousins, the elk and the deer
All three grow antlers on top of their ears
But moose grow the widest and the longest
The thickest, the toughest and the strongest

Bull moose use them to whack bushes and trees
Knocking off food like the berries and leaves
And moose will sometimes use their horns in a fight
Whacking each other with all of their might

The winners then chase the losers away
Or whack'em again if they want to stay
The biggest bull moose will most often win
But the losers might want to fight again

Moose like to live where the winters aren't nice
And the cold damp weather brings snow and ice
But they have thick skin and lots of thick hair
Which keeps them warm in the bitter cold air

Most moose have small beards that hang from the neck
If you call them scraggly, you'd be correct
It doesn't seem that they have a good use
But if you see one, you've just seen a moose.

N

NABARLEKS

Looking a lot like a small kangaroo
Nabarleks come from Australia too
These cute little kangaroo wanna-be's
Are also called Little-Rock Wallabys

They're about the size of a basketball
That's what we mean when we say they are small
Their kangaroo cousins on the other hand
Often grow up to be big as a man

Nabarleks hide in the bushes all day
They're cute, but they're shy and don't wanna play
They come out at night when it's not so hot
To find grass and leaves which they eat a lot

They usually leap when they move around
Quick, but quiet, hardly making a sound
They have strong hind legs and soft padded feet
So they're hard to hear when they go to eat

They'll take silent jumps like a great big cat
Who's sneaking to catch a bird or a rat
But nabarleks won't chase animal pests
Or scare them out of their burrows and nests

All nabarleks want is to eat green stuff
Like grass and plants 'til they've eaten enough
Then they'll probably belch and drink some water
To keep their cool as the day gets hotter

When nabarleks belch and they surely do
They won't belch as loud as a kangaroo
That's 'cause they're shy and don't like to make noise
Not even the rudest nabarlek boys

NABARLEK
THEY'RE CUTE, BUT THEY'RE SHY

Nabarlek babies look cute and funny
Tucked in the pouch on their mommy's tummy
All you can see is their heads sticking out
As their bright brown eyes are looking about

A nabarlek's tail is easy to find
Sticking way out from its behind
Like an extra long leg out on the ground
To keep that nabarlek from falling down

Nabarleks have nice and pretty gray coats
With red and black on their tummies and throats
Petting that soft fur might seem to be fun
But if you touch it, they'll probably run

The next time you go to visit a zoo
Take the time to look at a kangaroo
'Cause nabarleks probably won't be there
They're not often in zoos or anywhere

They're very unhappy when they get caught
So people just leave them alone a lot
But they look like kangaroos after all
They're just shy and small as a basketball

So pretend that the kangaroo you see
Is so small its head comes up to your knee
You might even have to close your eyes
To think of a kangaroo that size

And as you pretend, you wouldn't be wrong
To think that this silly poem's too long.

NABARLEK BABIES LOOK CUTE AND FUNNY
TUCKED IN THE POUCH ON THEIR MOMMY'S TUMMY

OSTRICHES

Ostriches are great big weird looking birds
Some folks think that they're too goofy for words
They flap their big wings but you'll wonder why
They flap and they flap but they never fly

And here's a strange fact that might make you laugh
An ostrich is something like a giraffe
They both have long legs and run pretty fast
And long skinny necks and they both eat grass

And their long necks move their heads all around
Up high toward the sky or down to the ground
When their heads are up they can see real well
And down by the ground they can eat and smell

But when you see an ostrich up real close
You'll know that it looks like a bird the most
It's got feathers and wings but no one knows
Why each of its feet grows only two toes

Because most other birds have two times more
Yes, an ostrich has two where they have four
But ostriches run fast on those two-toed feet
With their long, strong legs they're just hard to beat

But they could go faster if they could fly
And when they flap their wings they seem to try
They often flap'em as they run about
But they never fly, you can have no doubt

It's an unhappy fact and it's too bad
And it could be why they look a bit sad
But you sometimes see them keep on trying
So you'd think they might have dreams of flying

OSTRICHES ARE GREAT BIG WEIRD LOOKING BIRDS

28

They might never fly but they sure can run
So fast they can beat almost anyone
They can always outrun the fastest man
Even if he runs as fast as he can

They can beat roadrunners and rabbits, too
And most of the animals in the zoo
But they'll seldom outrun a big fast horse
And any of the big fast cats, of course

Ostriches kick if they get in a fight
With their big strong legs and all of their might
And when they're fighting, they make a big fuss
Flapping their wings as they kick up the dust

But ostriches can be a lot of fun
And you could even go riding on one
They're the only two-legged animals
That folks can ride like horses and camels

Just sit up high on an ostrich's back
You can make it walk or run down a track
Or dance all around if you're in its pen
One side to the other and back again

Ostriches hatch from eggs like all birds do
Their shells crack open when they're ready to
But ostrich eggs are the biggest of all
About half the size of a soccer ball

Those eggs have to be humongous, you know
'Cause big ostrich babies need room to grow
They grow in those shells, fast as the dickens
And when they hatch, they're as big as chickens

Ostriches don't have teeth to chew their food
So they swallow it whole which might seem rude
They eat worms and seeds and lizards and plants
And all kinds of bugs like crickets and ants

YOU COULD EVEN GO RIDING ON ONE

29

OSTRICHES continued

But the bugs and plants, the worms and lizards
Get chewed up in the ostriches gizzards
And if you want to know just how gizzards chew
Just read the next verses and they'll tell you

An ostrich's gizzard looks like a sock
Down by its tummy and chock full of rocks
Yes, the ostrich eats rocks and pebbles, too
To fill up that gizzard so it can chew

The rocks then grind up what the ostrich eats
'Cause its gizzard works like a mouthful of teeth
In goes the food and the rocks grind it good
And it gets nice and gooey like chewed food should

We hope you will ride an ostrich some day
And think of this poem when you ride away
So you'll remember that an ostrich can't fly
And with you on its back, it won't even try.

YOU COULD EVEN GO RIDING ON ONE

P

PORCUPINES

Most people believe they will be just fine
If they never get near a porcupine
And you will probably believe so too
When you find out what touching one can do

They don't have fur, but grow long thick hairs
They're sticky and sharp and grow everywhere
So most people would rather eat a bug
Than ever give a porcupine a hug

People call those sharp hairs by different names
Such as spines or quills, but they're all the same
They're pointy and stiff and can stick your skin
And sting like a needle when one goes in

... 'SPINES OR QUILLS, BUT THEY'RE ALL THE SA

Porcupines grow up to be fairly big
Bigger than most cats, but smaller than pigs
Some live on the ground and others in trees
And with those sharp hairs, they go where they please

Porcupines eat a lot of salty stuff
They must love salt 'cause they can't get enough
They'll eat paint and plywood, and salty plants
Pickles and garbage and sweaty old pants

Anything salty will be a great treat
For porcupines wanting something to eat
They'll lick road salt from curbings and wires
And even chew holes in salty tires

And porcupines who live by the ocean
Must believe it's a wonderful notion
To slurp up the water down at the beach
So salty and wet and easy to reach

They like to go find food and drink at night
So they hide and snooze when the sun shines bright
They don't like to be seen much during the day
But they're not too pretty, so that's OK

Porcupines are found where the weather's nice
They don't like too much rain, or cold or ice
And they don't like places that get too hot
They just like to stay warm or cool a lot

Porcupines seem lonely and bashful and dumb
They can't be petted so they're not much fun
And if porcupine kids love their mothers
You'll wonder how they hug one another.

... SPINES OR QUILLS, BUT THEY'RE ALL THE SA

QUAILS

Quails are birds, they fly high but they're small
Not as wide as chickens and not as tall
But they might laugh when they soar through the sky
Because they all know that chickens can't fly

Girl quails are called hens and boys are called cocks
And bunches or groups are sometimes called flocks
But covey's the name that's most often heard
When people talk about groups of these birds

...Quails... COVEY'S THE NAME MOST OFTEN HEARD

But it's also OK to call coveys quails
Or if you like you can just call them quail
But quails never care what names you repeat
All they want to do is find stuff to eat

Quails eat insects and worms and seeds and grains
And love to hunt food just after it rains
'Cause then their food is all muddy and wet
Just floating around and easy to get

There are lots of places where quails are found
Some live up in trees, some close to the ground
Like most other birds, they always build nests
Where they lay their eggs and hang out and rest

You'll find some quail nests where there's lots of shade
Under bushes and trees in holes they've made
Which they fill up with grass, so soft and green
And change it often, so their nests stay clean

Those nests are quite big, and they have to be
Because quail hens lay lots of eggs, you see
They sometimes lay as many as twenty
Or more or less, but it's always plenty

The nest must have room for the family
For all of the eggs and their hen mommy
And the cock daddy who visits the hen
And might sleep over every now and then

Quail eggs are pretty and they are small
A little bigger than a ping pong ball
They're spotted in colors from brown to blue
And you can eat'em, 'cause they're good for you

When the eggs start hatching, the chicks come out
Tiny and scrawny and gawking about
But they grow up fast and soon comes the day
When they flap their wings and they fly away

Most quails have feathery growths on their heads
But people call them crests or crowns instead
If you see them on birds as they fly by
You can be sure they're quails 'cause you'll know why

CALIFORNIA QUAIL
...CRESTS OR CROWNS

If you want to see quails, it won't be hard
They might just fly over your back yard
And hang out in the parks or woods near you
Or be living happily at the zoo

Looking for quails can often be fun
'Cause you'll likely find many more than one
Even a bunch of a hundred or so
Which should be called a covey, as you know

They might be on the ground or in the air
Resting under a bush or anywhere
And we think you'll think, sure as the dickens
That quails are a lot more fun than chickens.

R

REINDEER

A reindeer's as big as a grown up horse
That's bigger than most other deer of course
And there's another name for reindeer too
It starts with a "C" and it's caribou

When you say reindeer, it's one you might mean
But you could mean nine or even nineteen
When you say caribou the same rule's true
You could mean one or one hundred and two

Reindeer or caribou, one or many
Just call'em the same if you ever see any
But we'll call'em reindeer in this silly verse
'Cause we think caribou sounds a bit worse

Most reindeer live where the weather's not nice
Where the wind blows the snow across the ice
Where icicles hang from the limbs of trees
And if you don't dress warmly, you might freeze

But reindeer don't mind 'cause they can keep warm
Staying out all day in the coldest storm
That's because they grow nice furry soft coats
Which keep out the cold, so they're warm as toast

Reindeer have horns that grow big and spread wide
Sticking way out from their heads on each side
All reindeer have them, both women and men
They fall off each year but grow back again

So they are called antlers, because of the fact
That when they fall off, they'll soon grow right back
But if you'd rather call'em horns instead
The reindeer won't care so go right ahead

Reindeer like to walk, they don't sit around
They walk through the woods, but not through the towns
They'll walk and walk more, many miles each day
Looking for food as they go on their way

They eat stuff that grows on the trunks of trees
They love it and eat as much as they please
It's called moss, it's green and easy to chew
But reindeer like it more than people do

They also eat grass and other green stuff
They'll chomp and they'll chew till they've had enough
Then they might find some big mushrooms to eat
And even some bird eggs for a nice treat

Yes, reindeer are always eating a lot
They live where it's cold and never gets hot
They walk in cold wind and when it's snowing
And need full tummies to keep on going

Reindeer feet are small and don't grow a toe
People call them hooves and that you should know
One foot's a hoof but it's hooves if there's more
And everyone knows a reindeer has four

If reindeer could talk they would say "No way"
They could fly anywhere with Santa's sleigh
And they sure couldn't walk with it fast enough
For Santa to bring all the presents and stuff

But reindeer can't talk and they really don't know
Just what it is that makes Santa's sleigh go
Or if there's a reindeer whose nose can glow.

S

SKUNKS AND SKINKS

This poem is about the skunk and the skink
One likes to slither, the other to stink
Two weird animals, whose names start with "S"
Do different weird things, as you might have guessed

The skunk will stink as it's walking around
While the skink slithers around on the ground
The skunk looks like a big black and white cat
But the snake-like skink doesn't look like that

So we'll tell about the stinky skunk first
Of all the animals it smells the worst
And when we're done, we will tell about skinks
And hope you don't think that this poem stinks

A skunk blows stink from its rear in a spray
To make other animals stay away
They get a whiff of it and run off quick
'Cause too much of a whiff can make them sick

Skunks don't care a bit where that stinky spray goes
So sometimes it gets on a person's clothes
Which will ruin them 'cause there's not much doubt
That there's just no way to wash the stink out

If skunks didn't stink you might think they're cute
But they just don't care, they don't give a hoot
They're grumpy and mean, they're not nice and kind
And they'll eat any darned thing they can find

They'll eat garbage and rats and birds and bees
And all of the worms and bugs that they please
They'll also eat nuts and berries and plants
And old rotten fruit that's covered with ants

SKUNK

Yes, they look kind of cute, but they're no fun
And you wouldn't ever want to catch one
So now let's talk about skinks for a change
They smell OK, but they are a bit strange

Skinks have big heads, but their legs are quite small
And some skinks don't have any legs at all
But their legs don't have to be big and strong
"Cause they don't need'em to slither along

But most skinks will have a tail and that's a fact
And if it comes off it will grow right back
If you saw a skink's tail you might say "gee whiz"
'Cause it's longer than a skink's body is

The tail starts out wide but soon gets narrow
Sort of like a skinny, floppy arrow
And the skink can waggle it back and forth
Toward the west, the east, the south or the north

They can use their tails to twist and push
As their bellies slide through the rocks and bush
But the skinks that have legs can crawl and walk
Straight up a steep wall or over a rock

The biggest skinks are about a foot long
Which would be twelve inches if we're not wrong
But most skinks would be quite a bit smaller
About the length of a paper dollar

Some folks call skinks lizards and that's okay
They're a lot like lizards in many ways
But true lizards have longer legs and necks
So for skinks the name skink is more correct

MANY SKINKS ARE BROWN

And remember that skinks are not all the same
The big ones and small ones all have that name
Some crawl, walk and climb and some have no legs
Some have live babies while others lay eggs

SKUNKS AND SKINKS continued

Some skinks have spots which are both large and small
And some do not have any spots at all
Many skinks are brown, some are white and grey
So they're really not all the same, no way

A skink will eat any thing that can crawl
Worms, mice and crickets, so long as they're small
Snails and beetles, any bug they can find
You would think they'd taste bad, but skinks don't mind

So now you know something about the skink
And also the skunk which has a big stink
But now that you know, we're willing to bet
You wouldn't want either one as a pet.

SKUNK

MANY SKINKS ARE BROWN

T

TIGERS

You've probably seen tigers on TV
And in books like this, they're easy to see
And you may have seen tigers at the zoo
And showing off at a circus or two

Tigers are cats you won't have in your house
They're too big and strong and won't chase a mouse
They'd hang out in the kitchen stealing your meat
Raw, cooked or frozen, they'd snag it to eat

Yes, tigers are strong and they can run fast
But they soon get pooped so their runs don't last
One could outrun a deer for a rather short bit
But then run out of breath and have to quit

Tigers can also go jumping along
In leaps and bounds because their legs are strong
They can jump about twenty feet and then
They could rest a minute and jump again

Most animals can't jump like tigers do
Not even jackrabbits or kangaroos
There might be others that can jump as far
But we just don't know who and where they are

Most folks think that tigers act like they're proud
Their posture is good and their growls are loud
The girl tigers are smaller than the boys
And the boys growl louder and make more noise

When they see tigers most animals run
Because they think tigers aren't much fun
They know a tiger might want to catch'em
And if one does it might bite and scratch'em

TIGERS CAN ALSO GO JUMPING ALONG

Tigers are quite handsome, and fun to see
But they might run off so they can't run free
That's why the best place for tigers to stay
Is a nice place where they can't get away

Nice zoos are places where they live with ease
Where they eat lots of meat and do as they please
But circus tigers really do a lot
When they show off all the tricks they've been taught

There are wild tigers and they are at home
In far away jungles where they can roam
And creep around on their quiet cat feet
When they're out looking for something to eat

NICE ZOOS ARE PLACES WHERE THEY LIVE WITH EASE

And they love to swim in rivers and ponds
They'll dive in and paddle and soon be gone
And in summer when the weather's hotter
They might play all day in the cool water

Tigers are the biggest cats that are known
They've got big muscles and humongous bones
Some will grow to be nine feet long and then
They'll weigh about the same as three grown men

So tigers are big and handsome and proud
They're fast and they're strong and their growls are loud
And if they saw Tony, they might say "how come
People make that tiger look so dumb?"

U

UAKARIS pronounced "wuh KARR ees"

We'll tell you now of the uakari
When you say it, it should rhyme with "sorry"
Let's try it again now: say "wuh karr ee"
If you get it right, you won't be sorry

Uakaris have funny surprising heads
There's no hair there and the skin's bright red
Their faces are red and their ears are too
They're like hairless clowns when they look at you

Those bright red faces are easy to see
Even when they're sitting up in a tree
And trees are uakaris' favorite places
'Cause they're just like monkeys with red faces

They've got strong arms and legs like monkeys do
And shaggy coats of hair like monkeys too
But a true monkey has a hairy head
Not a red faced and hairless one instead

Uakaris eat stuff that grows in those trees
The fruit and the nuts and the nice green leaves
They swing just like monkeys from tree to tree
Grabbing lots to eat 'cause the food is free

And they like to sleep in the trees at night
Way up high on a limb and out of sight
The trees they like best are close to water
'Cause when daytime comes it might get hotter

They can then jump in to get cool and wet
And wash 'till they're clean as they want to get
And then they might take a cool drink or two
'Cause they can get thirsty the same as you

Most monkeys must think uakaris are small
They never get much more than three feet tall
Their short bodies look like big balls of hair
While their bald red heads stick up in the air

UAKARI THOSE BRIGHT RED FACES ARE EASY TO SEE

UAKARIS EAT STUFF THAT GROWS IN THOSE TREES

They like each other and hang out in groups
And each of those groups should be called a troop
Some big uakari troops will have dozens
Of families and their friends and cousins

When they call each other, they'll grunt and bellow
Long and short sounds both ugly and mellow
And they'll screech and scream when they're scared or mad
Or sob, groan and moan when they're tired or sad

Uakaris live where most folks haven't gone
By a huge river called the Amazon
In big wet jungles where it's green all year
With lots of animal voices to hear

You can find the Amazon if you look
In most any good geography book
Brazil's the country that it's mostly in
So first find that country then look again

Some zoos have uakaris, but not many
And most zoos never ever have any
Uakaris in zoos mostly sit and pout
And seem very happy when they get out

They love to hang out with friends in the trees
In their jungle home as free as the breeze
They can play and eat in the nice warm sun
And kick back to snooze when the day is done.

V

VOLES (and Moles)

If you know someone who knows about voles
They'll probably also know about moles
That's 'cause people find voles where moles are found
In tunnels and holes they've dug in the ground

Voles are small, and one might fit in your shoe
And if you've got big feet, one shoe might hold two
Voles might be small, but they work really hard
Digging their tunnels in gardens and yards

They dig those tunnels where the plant roots grow
Which they eat lots of as digging they go
The small tunnels voles dig criss-cross the ground
And moles dig big holes that just go straight down

So voles dig tunnels and moles dig big holes
But moles also dig small tunnels like voles
So moles dig more dirt and now you can guess
Which one of the two makes more of a mess

People think that voles look a lot like mice
And most folks believe that neither are nice
So most people don't want'em in the house
No way, never, not a vole or a mouse

But moles get bigger than voles ever do
So don't try to fit a mole in your shoe
They're about the size of a grown-up cat
So a mole might fit inside of your hat

But that's not where you'd want a mole to be
'Cause they're usually quite filthy, you see
They stay in their holes and tunnels all day
All covered with dirt and digging away

VOLES DIG THOSE TUNNELS WHERE THE PLANT ROOTS GROW

Voles and moles don't always eat the same stuff
Voles gobble up plants like they can't get enough
But moles eat earthworms, a lot of 'em too
And that's not something any vole would do

Voles don't like worms, but they often eat bugs
And creepy critters like snails and slugs
And when voles chew big holes in a tree trunk
Folks might think those holes were chewed by a skunk

Yes, voles dig around in the dirt all day
So they're probably too busy to play
And here's a fact that might make you squirm
Moles like to stay in their holes and eat worms

This poem was meant to be about voles
But then it, somehow, got mixed up with moles
And there's even some mice in one dumb verse
And also a skunk which just makes it worse.

MOLES EAT EARTHWORMS,
A LOT OF 'EM TOO

W

WALRUSES

Walruses live in the ice and the snow
Up by the North Pole where the cold winds blow
They hang out all day on big blocks of ice
Which may seem crazy, but they think it's nice

They keep warm 'cause they grow huge coats of fat
You'd stay warm too with a big coat like that
Those fatty coats grow just under their skin
And that's why walruses never look thin

WALRUSES ... HANG OUT ALL DAY ON BIG BLOCKS OF ICE

We don't know why, but that fat's called blubber
And it feels like thick and gooey rubber
It covers the walrus, both front and back
And from head to tail like a squishy sack

Walruses are all quite pudgy and big
Each one weighs more than a humongous pig
Some walruses weigh four-thousand pounds
That's two blubbery tons to haul around

And lots of 'em grow to be twelve feet long
That's four yards of blubber if we're not wrong
They're roly-poly like big bags of goo
They've got rough brown skin and their hair's short, too

And each walrus grows two long teeth that match
They're called tusks and they're used to dig and scratch
They grow down past the jaw, one on each side
Like huge white whiskers the walrus can't hide

They scratch and dig with those tusks in the ice
Making messy holes which do not look nice
But walruses love'em because they're used
To flop in and take a big walrus snooze

They've got weird faces and funny beards too
Which look more like brushes than most beards do
Their noses look smashed and their ears are small
They've got sideways eyes and their heads are bald

But walruses must think they look OK
They hang out together in groups all day
They'll loaf on the ice, then go for a swim
Boys and girls together, they'll dive right in

They swim in water that's too cold for you
So don't jump in 'cause you'd freeze and turn blue
It's icy water that's colder than snow
But walruses will just dive in and go

And, that's because of their blubbery coats
Which cover them up so they're warm as toast
They'll swim around for an hour or two
Finding food to put in their mouths and chew

Walruses will open their mouths up wide
To scoop up some shells which have clams inside
And then suck the clams right out of those shells
Which is something people can't do too well

Walruses love clams, but like more to eat
They think shrimps and crabs can be a nice treat
They'll gobble up snails and worms by the bunch
There are lots of things they might have for lunch

When looking for food, a walrus dives down
Deep in the water where good stuff is found
It can go down hundreds of feet and then
Pop up to the top and dive down again

WHEN LOOKING
FOR FOOD A WALRUS
DIVES DOWN

Or when it pops up, if it wants to stay
And float around for the rest of the day
It will blow up an airbag in its throat
Which will help that walrus kick back and float

There's much more about walruses to tell
Like the noises they make and how they smell
But this poem's already gone on too long
So this is the end of the walrus song.

XERUS

Here's an animal whose name starts with X
It's probably one that no one expects
And you say it like it starts with a Z
It's "zeerus" you say when XERUS you see

In fact, it's Z not X that's often heard
If that X goes first when you spell a word
Xerox, xylophone, xerography too
Xilose and xylem, they're just a few

And when you say xerus, what you could mean
Could be just one or ten thousand nineteen
'Cause for any number of them you choose
There's just one word, xerus, that you can use

A dictionary will have many more
Which you probably haven't heard before
But this is a xerus poem, that's all
It's not about xenias or xylitol

Or another X word that you might find
It's just about xerus if you don't mind
They're like little squirrels that dig in the ground
To make the small holes in which they are found

Yes, they look like squirrels, but they don't climb trees
Which the real squirrels do as much as they please
So down on the ground on their little feet
Xerus hop about finding stuff to eat

They'll gobble seeds and grains, bird eggs and fruits
Grasshoppers and field mice, bean pods and roots
They'll hop around and eat most every day
But at night they'll go to their holes and stay

XERUS GOBBLE BEAN PODS AND ROOTS

Xerus live in groups of twenty or more
So each one has another hole next door
In fact there's lots of close neighbors around
Each in their own hole in a xerus town

Those holes are connected to each other
So xerus go visit one another
When they go visit, they'll usually stroll
In the tunnels they've dug from hole to hole

Most xerus don't live in the U.S.A.
But in Africa, which is far away
And you won't find them in many zoos
So we hope this poem is helpful to you

SO XERUS GO VISIT ONE ANOTHER

In some ways, xerus are like jackrabbits
They've both got many of the same habits
They eat the same stuff and hop on the ground
And hide in their holes when the sun goes down

Some folks think xerus make cute little pets
But most farmers think they're bad little pests
It's fun to watch them coming and going
But they'll steal food that farmers are growing

Their backsides are tan and their tummies are white
And those long xerus tails make quite a sight
They're cute and fuzzy and they stick way out
From xerus behinds as they go about

Some mornings xerus just lie in the sun
Resting on their tummies, it must be fun
They might snooze there until it's time for lunch
And then start looking for some food to munch

Munching and resting and snoozing away
That's how most xerus like to spend their day
They seem quite happy and to have no cares
So we hope your days are pleasant like theirs.

Y

'CAUSE YOU CAN RIDE ON THE BACK OF A YAK

'CAUSE YOU CAN MILK A YAK, IF YOU KNOW HOW

MOST YAKS LIVE IN TALL MOUNTAINS, THAT IS TRUE

YAKS

Some folks think yak means a lot of talking
But real yaks don't talk, they just go walking
They're animals which you should know of course
And each one's big as a cow or a horse

And a yak's like a horse and that's a fact
'Cause you can ride on the back of a yak
And it's a fact that a yak's like a cow
'Cause you can milk a yak if you know how

The mountains most live on are very high
Reaching a mile or more up in the sky
They feel best up high in that mountain air
'Cause for them, it's the best air anywhere

The high mountain lands where most yaks hang out
Are in Asia which you may know about
They're called Himalayas, and if you look
You'll find'em in a geography book

Most yaks live in tall mountains, that is true
But you can find yaks, too, in many a zoo
And some of those zoos aren't up high, no way
But their yaks look fine and they eat okay

Like horses and cows, yaks eat hay and grass
And moss from the trees and rocks that they pass
The horses and cows pig out on that stuff
But yaks don't eat more when they've had enough

Yaks are calm and friendly, useful and smart
You can ride'em and they will pull a cart
They can learn their names and come when you call
And when the weather's cold, they don't care at all

Yaks are also used to carry big loads
On mountainsides where there aren't any roads
For many miles where it's rocky and rough
Yaks go with their loads, cause they're strong and
tough

The food folks make from yak milk tastes swell
They eat it or put it in boxes to sell
Yak milk makes butter and yogurt and cheese
And, yes, those folks eat as much as they please

Yak boys are called bulls, the girls are called cows
And the bulls and the cows are each other's pals
They hang out together most of the day
When they don't have a load to carry away

Bulls weigh more than cows by hundreds of pounds
But they look alike and make the same sound
You'd know that sound if you've heard it before
It's like a grunt, not a moo or a roar

And every yak has two kinds of long hair
Which is used to make stuff, but yaks don't care
Their soft belly hair makes clothing and flags
The stiff hair from their backs makes ropes and bags

Both bulls and cows have a big pair of horns
Which don't grow out until after they're born
But only cows can give the milk yaks make
If you think bulls can, you've made a mistake

Yaks hear real well and their eyes are great, too
So if you go see'em, they can see you
And they'll remember, so if you come back
You might find some old friends among the yaks.

Z

ZEBRAS

Here's this book's last poem, don't read it too fast
Zebra starts with "Z", that's why it is last
So don't look for the next poem when you're done
'Cause we're sorry to say there won't be one

Zebra's an animal that's fun to know
It looks all dressed up and ready to go
With black and white stripes that cover its hair
From its front to its rear and everywhere

They go from its nose to above its eyes
And they're on its ears, is that a surprise?
Stripes are on its neck and even the hair
That grows out of its neck up toward the air

That straight strip of striped hair is called a mane
And we don't know why it has a strange name
There's stripes on its tummy, its legs and back
Everywhere you look, you see white and black

But this zebra story won't be complete
'Till we tell how they live and what they eat
And whether they're used to ride and pull loads
Like horses and mules on trails and roads

And there's some other stuff for us to tell
Like how well zebras hear and see and smell
And how they like to walk and trot and run
And how you can tell when they're having fun

Africa is known as the zebra's home
It has a lot of room for them to roam
In grassy meadows and other places
That have many empty open spaces

But there are zebras in the U.S.A.
That came from Africa, so far away
And found the grassy homes they love in zoos
Where they can roam and eat or take a snooze

A zebra eats like a horse or a mule
They think a lot of different plants are cool
They'll love it if it grows and if it's green
And they gobble grass like mowing machines

THERE'S STRIPES ON ITS TUMMY,
ITS LEGS AND BACK

But plants, grass and leaves are all that they eat
You'll never find one who likes to eat meat
And many strong, happy zebras are found
Who only eat greens that grow in the ground

Zebras have been used like horses in fact
Folks have jumped on'em to ride on their backs
And, yes, zebras have pulled wagons and carts
But they don't seem to think working is smart

It makes them all nervous and scared and sad
And sometimes it might even make them mad
So zebras don't work, they just hang around
Loafing and eating the green stuff they've found

Zebras can trot but think walking's more fun
And only if chased will a zebra run
But they are most likely to use their feet
Walking around looking for stuff to eat

They hang out in groups of thirty or so
And the groups are called herds if you'd like to know
All kinds of zebras hang out together
In friendly herds in all kinds of weather

THEY HANG OUT IN GROUPS...

Their eyes are good and they know each other
Father and mother, sister and brother
Aunts, uncles and cousins, all black and white
Can go find each other, both day and night

ZEBRAS continued

Zebras' make a long, loud, horn-honking noise
The girls can hear it and so can the boys
But loud noise is not all zebras can hear
They can hear whispers 'cause they have good ears

Zebras also smell well with their noses
From stinky stuff to beautiful roses
If something's trying to hide in the woods
Zebras might find it, 'cause their smelling's good

When a zebra's mad and trouble is near
It will point its ears back toward its rear
And when it's frightened of something instead
It will point its ears out straight ahead

But when it's happy and having some fun
It will point those ears up toward the sun
And if you've been happy with this small book
You might invite your friends to take a look.

SPECIAL NOTICE TO THE ABSENT ANIMALS

We're sorry we did not include you in this book. The animals we did include are choices we made, always meaning to be fair. But we certainly didn't even think of many animals we could have included if there had been enough room. So we understand if you are a little sad about being left out. We're a little sad too, and we often think of you.

Be proud that you are part of the World's Wonderful Animal Kingdom. We may write some more of these poem-stories in the future, so keep your eyes open. We always pray that your lives will be pleasant. And you should know that we know that we, ourselves, are also part of that Wonderful Animal Kingdom. We are all in this together.

Tom Guy Pettit   Peter O'Malley Pierson

Special thanks to Sharon Strong, Toby Willaby, Jessica Scarffe, Sloane and Lynn Pettit for the advice, help and encouragement. They were with us all the way.